# WISCONSIN

by Patricia Lantier

GARETH**STEVENS**

PUBLISHING

A Member of the WRC Media Family of Companies

Please visit our web site at: www.garethstevens.com
For a free color catalog describing Gareth Stevens Publishing's
list of high-quality books and multimedia programs, call
1-800-542-2595 (USA) or 1-800-387-3178 (Canada).
Gareth Stevens Publishing's fax: (877) 542-2596.

Library of Congress Cataloging-in-Publication Data

Lantier, Patricia, 1952-
    Wisconsin / Patricia Lantier.
      p. cm. — (Portraits of the states)
    Includes bibliographical references and index.
    ISBN-10: 0-8368-4638-9   ISBN-13: 978-0-8368-4638-6 (lib. bdg.)
    ISBN-10: 0-8368-4657-5   ISBN-13: 978-0-8368-4657-7 (softcover)
    1. Wisconsin—Juvenile literature.  I. Title.  II. Series.
  F581.3.L36   2005
  977.5—dc22                                        2005042610

Updated edition reprinted in 2007. First published in 2006 by
**Gareth Stevens Publishing**
A Weekly Reader Company
1 Reader's Digest Rd.
Pleasantville, NY 10570-7000  USA

Copyright © 2006 by Gareth Stevens, Inc.

Editorial direction:  Mark J. Sachner
Project manager:  Jonatha A. Brown
Editor:  Betsy Rasmussen
Art direction and design:  Tammy West
Picture research:  Diane Laska-Swanke
Indexer:  Walter Kronenberg
Production:  Jessica Morris and Robert Kraus

Picture credits:  Cover, p. 4 © Diane Laska-Swanke; p. 5 © Corel; pp. 6, 29
© James P. Rowan; p. 8 © MPI/Getty Images; pp. 10-11 © Library of Congress;
pp. 12, 15, 16, 17, 20, 25 © Gibson Stock Photography; p. 22 © PhotoDisc;
p. 24 Donald S. Abrams/Wisconsin Department of Tourism; p. 27 Doug
Alft/Wisconsin Department of Tourism; p. 28 © Scott Boehm/Getty Images

Printed in the United States of America

2 3 4 5 6 7 8 9 09 08 07

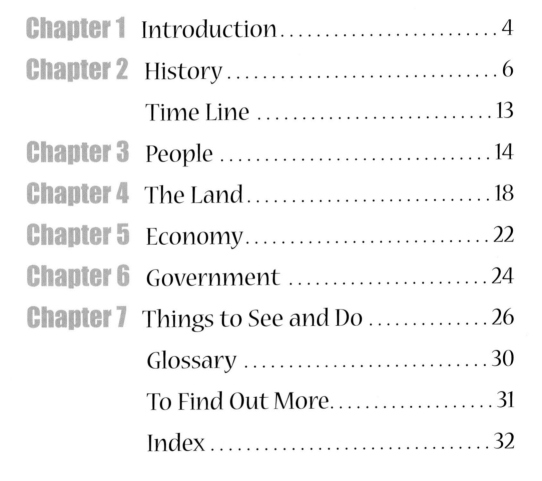

Words that are defined in the Glossary appear
in **bold** the first time they are used in the text.

On the Cover: The Milwaukee Art Museum holds more than twenty thousand works of art. The museum is a shining jewel on Lake Michigan's shore.

# Introduction

If you could visit Wisconsin, where would you go? Circus World Museum? Wisconsin Dells? Milwaukee? Wisconsin has many fun places to visit.

Wisconsin has different weather in each of the four seasons. People can enjoy sports, festivals, and other activities in every season.

The state also has a rich history. People moved to Wisconsin from many countries around the world. They worked together to make the state an exciting place to live and visit.

Wisconsin has something for everyone!

Farms, especially dairy farms, always have been an important part of Wisconsin's way of life.

# WISCONSIN
## 1848

**The state flag of Wisconsin.**

# WISCONSIN FACTS

- Became the 30th U.S. state:  May 29, 1848
- Population (2006):  5,556,506
- Capital:  Madison
- Biggest Cities:  Milwaukee, Madison, Green Bay, Kenosha
- Size:  54,310 square miles (140,663 square kilometers)
- Nickname:  The Badger State
- State Tree:  Sugar maple
- State Flower:  Wood violet
- State Animal:  Badger
- State Bird:  Robin

# History

Native Americans first came to Wisconsin thousands of years ago. They moved from lands farther west. These people lived by hunting large animals. Later, as the climate grew warmer, they gathered fruits, nuts, and rice. They also fished and learned to grow corn, squash, and beans. The rich **soil** in the area was just right for farming.

### Explorers and Settlers

People from France first came to Wisconsin in the 1600s. An explorer named Jean Nicolet landed on the shore of Lake Michigan in Green Bay in 1634. Two

**The Wisconsin River is the longest river in the state.**

other men, Louis Jolliet and Father Jacques Marquette, also came to Wisconsin. They explored the land and rivers in 1673.

Most of the first Europeans wanted to trade with the Natives for furs. Some wanted the Natives to become Christians. Priests moved to the area to build churches.

Green Bay was the first lasting European settlement in Wisconsin. In 1764, it was founded by Augustin Monet de Langlade. It became a place where Europeans and Natives could meet to trade.

## Time of War

People from Britain settled in **colonies** along the Atlantic coast of America. They had to follow British laws. But they wanted to

### A Mission of Peace

Explorer Jean Nicolet had a special job. France wanted him to find a way to China. He could make friends with the people of that country. Then, France could trade with the Chinese. Nicolet landed on the beach of Green Bay in Lake Michigan. He hoped he had found China. He dressed in a long **silk** robe to greet the people. The Native Americans of Wisconsin met Nicolet instead. The Natives were surprised by Nicolet's robe and by the two pistols he fired into the sky. Nicolet did not find China. But he did find a rich new land.

be independent. The Revolutionary War began in 1775. The colonists won the war. The colonies became the United States of America.

## Wisconsin Territory

New settlers in Wisconsin wanted to farm the land.

## FUN FACTS

### The Big Ice

A long time ago, most of Wisconsin was covered by huge pieces of ice called **glaciers**. Tall cliffs, rolling hills, and great lakes were left behind as the ice melted or moved away. Glaciers moving across the land formed the state's natural beauty.

They did not want to trap for furs. The settlers cut down forests to plant crops. They also built houses, roads, and towns. Some people mined for **lead**. In 1825, several Native tribes signed a **treaty**, or written agreement, with the U.S. government. This Treaty of Prairie du Chien ("Prairie of the Dog") caused the Natives to lose their land.

Wisconsin became known as Wisconsin **Territory** in 1836. Henry Dodge, a miner, was named governor of the new territory. In 1848, Wisconsin became the thirtieth state.

### Civil War

People began to argue over the issue of slavery.

In 1825, Native Americans from many tribes met with people from the U.S. government. They talked about how to divide the land.

8

## Famous People of Wisconsin

# Laura Ingalls Wilder

**Born:** February 7, 1867, Lake Pepin, Wisconsin

**Died:** February 10, 1957, Mansfield, Missouri

Laura Ingalls was born in Wisconsin. Her family lived in many places. They traveled in a covered wagon to several states. Laura became a teacher when she was only fifteen years old. After marrying Almanzo Wilder, she began writing. Laura's daughter asked her to write stories about her childhood. She wrote many stories and books, and she became famous. *Little House on the Prairie* is one of these books.

## IN WISCONSIN'S HISTORY

**Black Hawk's War**
Henry Dodge was a rich lead miner. He forced Native Americans off their land and made them move away. In 1832, a warrior named Black Hawk brought together a group of Natives. He led this group of about 1,000 people on a march. They wanted to live and hunt on their own land again. They were turned away and attacked by soldiers. Fewer than 150 Natives survived.

Northern states wanted to end slavery. Southern states wanted to keep slavery. The South broke away and formed its own country. People in the North wanted the country to stay together. The North fought against the South in the Civil War. The war lasted for four years. The North won, slavery ended, and the country stayed as one.

### A Time of Growth

Many more people moved to Wisconsin after the Civil

## FACTS

### What's in a Name?

Wisconsin was first named by Native Americans who lived there. Early French explorers spelled it different ways. The name *Wisconsin* may mean "grassy place." It also might mean "gathering of the waters" or "place of the beaver."

War. By 1880, most of the good land was being farmed. **Factories** were built to make machines and other products. These factories gave jobs to workers. But life was hard for many people. Some workers had to take jobs that were not safe. Some had to stay at work for too many hours each day. Many did not make enough money for all the time they spent at their jobs. Some workers united to form groups called unions to protect themselves. The unions helped workers get better working conditions and fewer hours at work.

### A New Century

Two big wars were fought in the first half of the twentieth

## FUN FACTS

### Christmas Tree Ship

A ship named *Rouse Simmons* was built in Milwaukee in 1868. For many years, it carried Christmas trees to the people of Chicago, Illinois. These trees came from the forests of northern Wisconsin. The ship's captain would deliver the trees at Thanksgiving. In 1912, the ship was caught in a winter storm. It sank to the bottom of Lake Michigan. It was not found again until 1971.

**The mineral galena is a major part of lead. The Cleveland Mine at Hazel Green, shown here in about 1915, produced galena.**

century. These wars took place in Europe and Asia. U.S. soldiers fought in both of these wars.

After the first war, selling beer and similar drinks was against the law in the United States. Thousands of people in Wisconsin had jobs making and selling beer. All these workers lost their jobs.

The **Great Depression** began in the early 1930s. During this time, the prices paid for goods fell. People all over the country lost their jobs. This meant even more people in Wisconsin were out of work. The state

CLEVELAND MINE HAZEL GREEN WIS.

**Wisconsin Dells is a favorite vacation spot for tourists and people who live in the state.**

thought of a plan to help. Each company had to save a little money for every person hired. If workers lost their jobs, the companies could pay them a while longer. Today, the whole country has a program that helps workers who lose their jobs.

## Today in Wisconsin

Wisconsin today has dairy farms, different businesses, and strong **communities**. It has good schools. People enjoy sports of all kinds. Caring for nature is important, and tourism is growing. In 2004, Gwen Moore from Milwaukee made history. She became the state's first African American member of Congress.

| | |
|---|---|
| **1634** | Explorer Jean Nicolet lands on the shore of Green Bay, Wisconsin. |
| **1673** | Louis Jolliet and Father Jacques Marquette explore the land and rivers in Wisconsin. |
| **1764** | Green Bay becomes the first lasting settlement in Wisconsin. |
| **1832** | Native American warrior Black Hawk leads more than 1,000 people back to land that was taken away from them. Fewer than 150 survive an attack from soldiers. |
| **1836** | The Wisconsin Territory is established. |
| **1848** | Wisconsin becomes the thirtieth state. |
| **1861–1865** | Wisconsin soldiers fight for the North during the Civil War. |
| **1918** | The United States makes the sale of beer and similar drinks illegal. This causes many people in Wisconsin to lose their jobs. |
| **1941** | U.S. involvement in World War II begins. |
| **2004** | Paul Hamm wins a gold medal in gymnastics at the summer Olympics. Gwen Moore is Wisconsin's first African American elected to Congress. |

# People

**M**ore than five million people live in Wisconsin. Native Americans were the first to live in the state. Settlers forced most of the Native tribes to move off their land. The settlers wanted to farm or mine. Today, the Native **population** is small but very proud of its history.

Most of Wisconsin's early settlers came from Europe. They came mainly from Germany and Norway. Later, people moved there from other parts of the world.

**Hispanics:** In the 2000 U.S. Census, 3.6 percent of the people living in Wisconsin called themselves Latino or Hispanic. Most of them or their relatives came from Spanish-speaking backgrounds. They may come from different racial backgrounds.

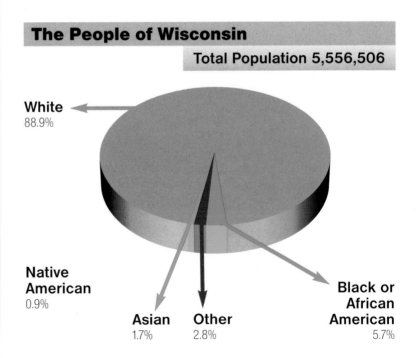

**The People of Wisconsin**

**Total Population 5,556,506**

White
88.9%

Native American
0.9%

Asian
1.7%

Other
2.8%

Black or African American
5.7%

Percentages are based on 2000 Census.

14

In the city of Milwaukee, homes, businesses, and boats line the Milwaukee River.

The state has many towns with fewer than one thousand people. Some people in these areas make a living by fishing, farming, or logging. Other towns are vacation places. People visit vacation places during all the seasons.

Most people in Wisconsin live in the southeastern part of the state. Settlers first moved there because the land was good for farming. The climate also was a little warmer than in the north.

Milwaukee is the largest city in the state. It is built on the shore of Lake Michigan. About six hundred thousand people live and work there.

All kinds of people live in Milwaukee. Many have ancestors from Germany, Poland, Italy, and Ireland.

## Famous People of Wisconsin

### Ringling Brothers

**Albert C. Ringling (1852–1916)**

**Otto Ringling (1858–1911)**

**Alfred T. Ringling (1861–1919)**

**Charles Ringling (1863–1926)**

**John Ringling (1866–1936)**

These five brothers were born in Baraboo. They began to sing and dance together in 1882. Two years later, they formed a small circus. The brothers toured with their circus in a few states. After a while, they bought their first elephant and started touring the entire country. They bought other small circuses to add to their own. In 1907, they bought the large Barnum & Bailey Circus. From then on, it was the biggest circus in the country.

But other people live there, too. Most African Americans in the state live in or near the city. So do many Native Americans and Latinos. People whose families moved to Wisconsin from other European and Asian countries also live there.

About two hundred thousand people live in Madison. It is the next largest city in the state. Many lawmakers live and work in Madison. Many students attend the university there.

The Circus Museum in Baraboo draws many visitors.

The main campus of the University of Wisconsin. It covers more than 900 acres (360 hectares). It has more than forty-one thousand students.

Wisconsin had the first kindergarten in the whole country. It opened in 1856 in Watertown.

## Education

People in the state believe in a good education. For a while, some churches had small schools. The first public school in the state opened in 1845. The University of Wisconsin was founded in 1848 in Madison.

## Religion

About 90 percent of the people in Wisconsin are Christians. Nearly 40 percent of these Christians are Catholics. Nearly 20 percent are Lutheran. Smaller numbers of people are Jews, Buddhists, and Muslims.

# The Land

**W**isconsin has many rivers and lakes. Hills, valleys, and plains cover large areas of land. Boulders and rocky cliffs add to the scenery. The state also has thick, green forests, most of which grow in the north. Glaciers formed most of the state's beauty. The highest point is Timms Hill. Timms Hill rises 1,951 feet (595 meters) above sea level.

## Climate

Wisconsin has long, cold winters. The summers are short and warm. The state receives about 30 inches (762 millimeters) of rain each year. The amount of snow the state receives during winter varies. The northern part of the state always has more snow than the southern part.

## Waterways

Wisconsin has about fifteen thousand lakes! Lake Winnebago is the biggest lake. Many people visit this lake for fishing and other water sports. Lake Michigan and Lake Superior form

## FUN FACTS

### Fun in the Dells

Wisconsin Dells is a vacation spot in the southern part of the state. Native American stories say a great snake once wiggled its way into this area. It carved a deep, narrow path in the land and rock. Water from the Wisconsin River filled this deep passage. It is lined with tall, rocky walls. Visitors can fish, camp, and take boat tours in summer. In winter, they can ski, swim in giant water parks, and go to haunted houses. Visiting the Dells is lots of fun.

# WISCONSIN

Keweenaw
Peninsula

Point Isabelle
Keweenaw Bay

Apostle
Islands NL

Outer
Island

Lake Superior

Point Abbaye

MINNESOTA

Bark
Point

Stockton
Island

MICHIGAN

N

Superior

Madeline
Island

W ● E

Saint
Croix NSR

S

Chequamegon NF

St Croix R.

L. Chippewa

Chippewa R.

Nicolet NF

Timms Hill

Lower Saint Croix NSR

Green Bay

Door Peninsula

● Chippewa Falls
● Eau Claire

● Wausau

Mississippi R.

Stevens Point ●

Green Bay ●

● Appleton

Wisconsin R.

L. Poygan

Petenwell L.

Oshkosh ●

L. Winnebago

● Manitowo●

La Crosse ●

Wisconsin Dells ●

Fond Du Lac ●

Sheboygan●

Beaver Dam ●

IOWA

Baraboo ●

● West Bend

Lake Michigan

Watertown ●

Wisconsin R.

Prairie du Chien ●

Madison ☆

● Milwaukee

## SCALE/KEY

0       50 Miles

Janesville ●

● Racine
● Kenosha

0   50 Kilometers

Beloit ●

⊛ State Capital

ILLINOIS

▲ Highest Point

Mountains

part of the **border** of the state. These are two of the largest freshwater lakes in the world.

The Wisconsin River is the longest river in the state. The Mississippi River forms part of the western edge of the state. It is the second-longest river in the country.

## Plants and Animals

Forests cover almost half the state. Maple, pine, and birch are some of the many kinds of trees that grow there. Wisconsin also has **prairies** with wild grasses. Prairies are areas of flat, grassy land. Many wildflowers grow in the state. The wood violet is the state flower.

| Major Rivers | |
| --- | --- |
| **Mississippi River** | 2,357 miles (3,792 km) long |
| **Wisconsin River** | 430 miles (692 km) long |
| **Chippewa River** | 183 miles (294 km) long |

**Country homes line the shore of Lake Mendota in Madison.**

## FACTS

### The Badger State

The badger is Wisconsin's state animal. It is short and stocky with a white stripe on top of its head. The badger has strong front limbs to dig for food and to make tunnels and **dens**. But the word *badger* also refers to the men who used to dig deep tunnels in the earth to mine for lead. In the old days, miners spent a lot of time in these holes.

Many kinds of birds live in Wisconsin. Loons live on northern lakes in the summer. They make loud, ghostly calls. Wild turkeys live in several parts of the state. Wisconsin's state bird is the robin. Robins visit the state in summer and move to warmer regions in winter.

Snakes, turtles, frogs, and lizards live in Wisconsin.

The yellow-bellied snake, also called a blue racer, is one of the fastest snakes in the country.

Lots of fish make their homes in the state's lakes. Trout, perch, bluegill, and bass are only some of them. The muskie is Wisconsin's state fish. Beavers and otters also live in Wisconsin's waters.

Foxes, snowshoe hares, black bears, coyotes, moose, and white-tailed deer live in Wisconsin. Squirrels and chipmunks also live here.

Several animals in the state are in danger of disappearing forever. Barn owls, ornate box turtles, northern ribbon snakes, and trumpeter swans are just a few of them. Now, special laws protect the homes and lives of these animals.

# Economy

The first Europeans who came to the state wanted animal furs. Native Americans traded and sold the furs. Later, mining made jobs for new settlers. Miners dug deep tunnels in the ground. Few people in the state still work in mining.

### Farming

Most of the first settlers in the area wanted to farm the rich land. The state still has many farms. Dairy farms produce milk and milk products. Wisconsin makes about one-fourth of the nation's cheese. Farmers in the state also grow sweet corn, green beans, cranberries, and peas.

Meatpacking is a big industry in the state. People around the country can enjoy tasty Wisconsin meats.

22

## Other Jobs

Some people in Wisconsin make a living by fishing and logging. Meatpacking also provides jobs. The state is known for its tasty hot dogs and sausages, as well as its cheese.

People also work in service jobs. Some are bankers, doctors, or teachers. Some sell houses or work at hotels. Others fix cars or work in places that sell food.

The southeastern part of the state has a lot of factories. Many people work in these factories to make tools, machines, and paper products. Wisconsin produces more paper than any other state. Also, a company in Wisconsin makes motorcycles that are sold around the world.

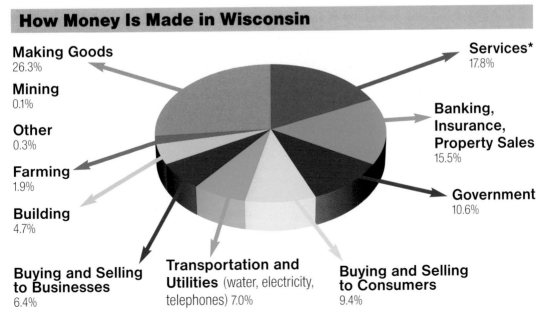

**How Money Is Made in Wisconsin**

**Making Goods**
26.3%

**Mining**
0.1%

**Other**
0.3%

**Farming**
1.9%

**Building**
4.7%

**Buying and Selling to Businesses**
6.4%

**Transportation and Utilities** (water, electricity, telephones) 7.0%

**Buying and Selling to Consumers**
9.4%

**Services***
17.8%

**Banking, Insurance, Property Sales**
15.5%

**Government**
10.6%

\* Services include jobs in hotels, restaurants, auto repair, medicine, teaching, and entertainment.

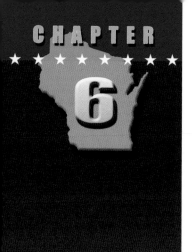

6

# Government

**M**adison is Wisconsin's capital city. The state's lawmakers work there. Wisconsin's government has three parts. They are the executive, legislative, and judicial branches.

### Executive Branch

The governor is head of the executive branch. This branch makes sure state laws are carried out. The lieutenant governor helps the governor. Other officials belong to the executive branch. Some are

The state capitol in Madison is built on a narrow strip of land between Lakes Monona and Mendota.

The lobby of the state capitol is decorated with paintings and materials that show the state's many resources.

elected, and some are chosen by the governor.

## Legislative Branch

The legislative branch makes state laws. The **legislature** has two bodies. It has a Senate and an Assembly. The Senate and the Assembly work together.

## Judicial Branch

Judges and courts form the judicial branch. Judges **interpret** the state's laws. They go to court when people are accused of crimes. Judges make sure everyone in trouble gets a fair trial. The highest court in Wisconsin is the supreme court.

## Local Government

Wisconsin is divided into seventy-two counties. A team of leaders elected by the people runs each county.

## WISCONSIN'S STATE GOVERNMENT

| Executive | | Legislative | | Judicial | |
|---|---|---|---|---|---|
| **Office** | **Length of Term** | **Body** | **Length of Term** | **Court** | **Length of Term** |
| Governor | 4 years | Senate (33 members) | 4 years | Supreme (7 justices) | 10 years |
| Lieutenant Governor | 4 years | Assembly (97 members) | 2 years | Appeals (16 judges) | 6 years |

# Things to See and Do

**P**eople in Wisconsin love fairs and festivals. The Holiday Folk Fair shows the dress, food, and music of the people who settled the state. Summerfest is a music festival in Milwaukee that lasts several days. It is one of the largest music festivals in the world. County fairs, church fairs, and other festivals take place all over the state.

The state's lakes are great for water sports. Many people like to swim, fish, and go boating in summer. Zoos and farm vacations also are fun. In winter, families can swim at indoor water parks, go ice skating, or enjoy the snow.

## Parks

Wisconsin has great natural beauty. The state has many parks where people can hike, ski, or just enjoy the view. Two national forests cover huge areas of land. These forests are great for camping, fishing, hiking, and more.

## FUN FACTS

### Holy Mustard!

The Mount Horeb Mustard Museum is famous. It has the largest mustard collection in the world — more than four thousand different kinds! The museum celebrates Mustard Day each year in August.

## Museums

The state has museums that are fun for the whole family. The Milwaukee Art Museum has thousands of works of art. It is more than one hundred years old.

Many museums are designed for kids. One of these museums has a small log cabin and fishing pond to explore. There also is a clown museum, a doll and toy museum, and a spinning top museum. In Milwaukee, Discovery World Museum is a special science center for young people. Betty Brinn Children's Museum, also in Milwaukee, is designed for kids ages ten and under.

## Sports

Wisconsin has many sports teams. It has big-league

World-famous Summerfest is set up on 75 acres (30 ha) along Lake Michigan in downtown Milwaukee. The festival features major musical entertainers and lasts for eleven days.

### FUN FACTS

**Golden Boy**

In 2004, the summer Olympics took place in Athens, Greece. Many U.S. athletes went to these games. Some were from Wisconsin. Paul Hamm from Waukesha won a gold medal in men's gymnastics.

football, basketball, and baseball teams. In football, the Green Bay Packers won the first two Super Bowls.

They won again in 1997. In baseball, the Milwaukee Brewers played in the 1982 World Series. The Milwaukee Bucks were the 1971 champions of the National Basketball Association.

Wisconsin has minor-league baseball teams, too. It also has soccer teams and hockey teams. The state's colleges also have many sports teams. These teams have thousands of fans.

**The Green Bay Packers are a respected and successful professional football team. Devoted fans paint their bodies or dress up in green and gold.**

## More Fun

If you live in Wisconsin or plan to visit, be sure to spend time in Door County for art shows and outdoor fun. The Wisconsin State Fair shows prize-winning farm animals. It also has music, rides, and delicious cream puffs. For two weeks every July, an aircraft show takes place in Oshkosh. People travel from all over the country to this event. You also may want to visit Circus World Museum.

## Famous People of Wisconsin

# Frank Lloyd Wright

**Born:** June 8, 1867, Richland Center, Wisconsin

**Died:** April 9, 1959, Phoenix, Arizona

Frank Lloyd Wright was an **architect** and writer. Some people think he was a **genius**. Mr. Wright did not like the designs of the houses and buildings around him. He dreamed of new designs and founded the Prairie School of Architecture. His homes and buildings are designed to suit the land around them. Many other architects have followed his example.

Peninsula State Park is part of Wisconsin's Door County Peninsula. Located along the Green Bay shores of Lake Michigan, the scenic park covers nearly 4,000 acres.

★ ★ ★ ★ ★ ★ ★ ★ ★ ★ ★ ★ ★ ★ ★ ★ ★ ★ ★ ★ ★ ★ ★ ★ ★ ★ ★ ★ ★

**architect** — a person who designs buildings

**border** — an edge or outer part

**colonies** — groups of people living in a new land but keeping ties with the place they came from

**communities** — groups of people who live near each other. These people often like to do many of the same things.

**dens** — hollow places where wild animals live

**genius** — a very smart person

**glaciers** — large bodies of ice that move across land

**factories** — buildings where goods and products are made

**Great Depression** — a time, in the 1930s when many people lost jobs and businesses lost money

**interpret** — to explain the meaning of something

**lead** — a white metal substance found in nature

**legislature** — a group that makes laws

**population** — the number of people who live in a place, such as a city, town, or state

**prairies** — large, grassy areas of land

**silk** — a soft, fine cloth

**soil** — earth; dirt

**territory** — an area that belongs to a country

**treaty** — a written agreement

## Books

*Frank Lloyd Wright for Kids.* Kathleen Thorne-Thomsen (Chicago Review Press)

*The Green Bay Packers Football Team.* Great Sports Teams (series). Arlene Bourgeois Molzahn (Enslow Publishers)

*Prairie Girl: The Life of Laura Ingalls Wilder.* William Anderson (HarperCollins)

*Song of the Circus.* Lois Duncan (Philomel Books)

*Wisconsin.* This Land Is Your Land (series). Ann Heinrichs (Compass Point Books)

*Wisconsin.* Rookie Read-About Geography (series). Lisa Trumbauer (Children's Press)

*Wisconsin: Facts and Symbols.* The States and Their Symbols (series). Emily McAuliffe (Franklin Watts)

## Web Sites

Circus World Museum
www.wisconsinhistory.org/circusworld

Eek! Environmental Education for Kids (Wisconsin)
www.dnr.state.wi.us/org/caer/ce/eek/index.htm

Wisconsin Kids Page
www.wisconsin.gov/state/core/kids_page.html

Wisconsin State Historical Society
www.wisconsinhistory.org

# INDEX